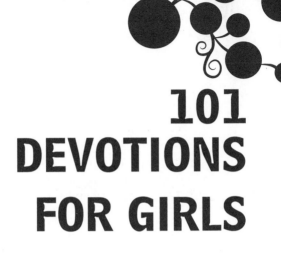

101 DEVOTIONS FOR GIRLS

From the Lives of
Great Christians

Copyright © Rebecca Davis 2017
ISBN: 978-1-78191-983-5
10 9 8 7 6 5 4 3 2 1

Published by Christian Focus Publications Ltd,
Geanies House, Fearn, Tain, Ross-shire
IV20 1TW, Scotland, UK.
Tel: 01862 871011
Fax: 01862 871699
www.christianfocus.com
email: info@christianfocus.com

Cover design by Tom Barnard
Printed and bound in China

101
DEVOTIONS
FOR GIRLS

From the Lives of Great Christians

REBECCA DAVIS

DAY 1

"I don't know what to do, Ann," Joy Ridderhof groaned to her friend. "I just worry all the time. I know it's because I want to do my best in my schoolwork, but oh, it gives me such a stomach-ache!"

"God will help you," Ann answered. "Ask Him to help."

"I always do," said Joy, "but nothing changes. I wish I could stop, but I know it's just because I want to do my best. Ohhh."

Was Joy right? Did worrying really just show that she wanted to do her best?

Jesus said in Matthew 6:34, "Therefore do not be anxious about tomorrow, for tomorrow will be anxious for itself. Sufficient for the day is its own trouble."

What Joy's worry really showed about her was that she wasn't trusting God. If she prepared and trusted God, she could be confident that He would help her do her best.

The same is true for you. If you're worrying about doing your best, in your schoolwork or any other area of life, it's time to stop worrying and start trusting the Lord.

***

Father, sometimes worrying seems like a natural thing to do. Help me to always remember that You're in control so I can trust You.

DAY 2

Joy heard a speaker who said that worrying meant a person's faith was small. He quoted George Mueller, who said, "The beginning of worry is the end of faith, and the beginning of true faith is the end of worry."

"True faith in the truly powerful God will bring an end to your worry," the speaker said. "He loves you! He can fill you with His joy!"

Joy had never thought about her worrying being a lack of faith. She had always thought it was a good thing! But now she repented and declared her trust in God.

Joy met the speaker, Robert McQuilkin, and became one of the first students at his Bible school. Then she went on to become a missionary, taking the gospel all over the world. There were many opportunities to worry, but Joy had learned that

every opportunity to worry was really an opportunity to trust.

***

Do not be anxious about anything, but in everything by prayer and supplication with thanksgiving, let your requests be made known to God. Philippians 4:6

Father, help me to remember that when I start worrying, I've stopped trusting. Help me to always trust instead of worrying.

DAY 3

Little baby Fanny Crosby was blinded by the foolish action of a man who said he was a doctor. Her young mother, Mercy, prayed and saved money for five years to take Fanny to a great doctor in New York City to see if he could help cure her eyes.

But the doctor examined Fanny's eyes and decided they couldn't be helped. Mercy was overcome with despair. She believed God hadn't heard her prayer.

When Mercy got home to her own mother, Fanny's grandma, she cried and could hardly be comforted. But Grandma knew God must have something good in store for Fanny.

Many years later, Fanny Crosby became world famous for the many hymns and gospel songs she wrote.

Very often when a heartbreaking thing happens we can only see the short perspective. But God's perspective is very different, and He is always working good, even in tragedy. We can trust Him.

***

And we know that for those who love God all things work together for good, for those who are called according to his purpose.
Romans 8:28

Thank You, Lord, that even when life is very hard or bad things happen, I can still trust You to work things out for good.

DAY 4

Young Amy Carmichael and her brothers were walking home from church one Sunday when they saw an old, frail woman carrying heavy bundles.

"I suppose we should help her," one of them muttered. They did it, but they didn't want to. Amy was horribly embarrassed to think that others were looking at her with this ugly, dirty old woman, carrying bundles! But a voice came to Amy, reminding her of words from 1 Corinthians.

Now if anyone builds on the foundation with gold, silver, precious stones, wood, hay, straw—each one's work will become manifest, for the Day will disclose it, because it will be revealed by fire, and the fire will test what sort of work each one has done. . . . If anyone's work is burned up, he will suffer loss. . . . 1 Corinthians 3:12-15

Amy knew what God was saying to her. She did this work only because she thought

she "ought" to, not out of a heart of love for God, so this work wasn't really pleasing to God.

Have you ever done any Christian work for the wrong reason? When the love of Christ pours into you, it can pour out to others. You can work for Him for the right reason.

***

Lord, help me to be aware of how I might be doing right only out of duty. Help me to do right because of the work You're working in me.

DAY 5

A lady named Mrs. Nicholl had promised God when she was young to become a missionary, but she never did. Instead of going to Bible school, she married a non-Christian man and began having children. But she repented of turning away from God, and cried out for the Lord to restore to her "the years the locust had eaten." She asked Him to call one of her children to be a missionary.

That lady's prayer was answered when her daughter, Margaret, became a missionary in Africa. Margaret sent letters to her mother about the great work God was doing in Africa, and Mrs. Nicholl's heart was turned from sadness to great joy. The years that she had wasted in disobedience had been restored.

We can trust God to do this, when we repent of turning away and instead turn fully to Him. Though there will be sadness

because of our sin, there can also be great joy because of His faithfulness.

***

I will restore to you the years that the swarming locust has eaten, the hopper, the destroyer, and the cutter, my great army, which I sent among you. Joel 2:25

Lord, show me when I go astray from Your ways. Help me to see that even though there will be sorrow because of sin, I can trust You to restore joy.

DAY 6

The missionary spoke at the small Bible school. "These tribal people of New Guinea are living in darkness," he said. "Who will go and tell them about eternal life in Jesus Christ?"

Several of the students who sat listening, young men and women, leaned forward to listen. They knew they wanted to go.

They didn't know it, but many of these tribal people had ancient strange prophecies, "Someday someone will come who will bring" . . . *something good.* Something that would last forever.

When the students finally went to New Guinea, they brought what the tribal people's ancient sayings had prophesied: eternal life. Many of the tribal people believed.

Maybe someday you'll take the gospel to someone who has never heard. It will be very hard, but it will be a great adventure. How will

these people hear the Good News of Jesus Christ unless someone tells them? Maybe that someone will be you.

***

How then will they call on him in whom they have not believed? And how are they to believe in him of whom they have never heard? And how are they to hear without someone preaching? Romans 10:14

Heavenly Father, show me if You want me to take the gospel to a foreign land. Thank You for people who are faithfully doing that now, telling others about Jesus.

DAY 7

No one knew what to do with the wild woman, so they chained her to rocks in the desert. Then they called Mary Bird, a missionary to that part of Persia (now called Iran) in the late 1800s.

"Lord Jesus," she prayed, "You delivered the demonized man. I know You are the same powerful God today."

Mary spent hours with the wild woman, praying over her, singing over her, loving her, and talking to her about Jesus. Before long, the wild woman was in her right mind. "My people deserted me," the woman said. "But you helped me."

"That was the power of Jesus Christ," said Mary. "He healed you."

"He is powerful," said the woman. "Jesus is the true God."

Do you believe Jesus is able to deliver people today the way He did in Bible times?

He's doing it, all over the world. He's looking for people of faith to trust Him and go forward in His work.

***

The seventy-two returned with joy, saying, "Lord, even the demons are subject to us in your name!" Luke 10:17

Lord Jesus, You are the God of powerful and mighty works. Use me to do them too!

DAY 8

How would Joy Ridderhof get all the way from California to South Carolina to go to Bible school? But Mr. McQuilkin, the founder of the Bible school, had said, "The Lord will guide you," so instead of worrying about it, Joy trusted God. Much to her surprise, her sister offered to pay her way.

Joy hadn't worried about it! She had trusted God! And the Lord had done it!

When the Lord called her to go to South America as a missionary, how would all the details come together? But instead of worrying, Joy trusted God, and she saw Him do that work too.

For the next fifty years Joy trusted God in all the many hard things that she did in her ministry work with Gospel Recordings. When things were hard—which they often were!—instead of worrying, she rejoiced.

God continued to show Himself strong, and the Word of God went forth with power.

***

I will rejoice and be glad in your steadfast love, because you have seen my affliction; you have known the distress of my soul.
Psalm 31:7

Lord Jesus, You are the Good Shepherd and Provider. Show me how I can choose the good that You have for me and rejoice in it.

DAY 9

Eight-year-old Fanny Crosby cried with discouragement, not so much because she was blind, but because she believed her blindness meant she would never be able to learn to read.

Grandma took her on her lap. "Fanny, if you pray with a humble heart to the God of your salvation, He will answer your prayer. If He answers it with a "No," it is because He has a better plan for you."

Fanny did pray, and then she wrote her first poem. The first part said,

Oh what a happy child am I!
Although I cannot see,
I am resolved that in this world
Contented I will be.

Sometimes it seems hard to be content when you have real problems in your life. It seems that God should take the problems away.

But keep trusting Him. If He doesn't remove the problems, it's because He has something better in mind, like He did for Fanny Crosby.

***

But he said to me, "My grace is sufficient for you, for my power is made perfect in weakness." Therefore I will boast all the more gladly of my weaknesses, so that the power of Christ may rest upon me.
2 Corinthians 12:9

Thank You, Lord, that You can use even my weakness as strength. Help me to trust in the power of Christ every day.

DAY 10

In the town of Belfast, Ireland, in the 1800s, many girls worked in the textile mills, making thread or cloth.

It was hard, dirty work, and the girls were paid so little they barely had enough to survive. They couldn't even afford to wear hats to church on Sundays, so instead they covered their heads with shawls. Some people scorned these "shawlies" and thought they weren't worth talking to.

But not Amy Carmichael. She knew the souls of the shawlies were every bit as valuable as the souls of any rich person, and she knew they needed the Lord. Amy loved them and taught them the Bible and prayed for them to grow to be Christ-like girls. The lives of many girls were changed.

What is your attitude toward girls who are different from you? No matter how different they are, you can love them and talk to them about Jesus.

***

Listen, my beloved brothers, has not God
chosen those who are poor in the world to
be rich in faith and heirs of the kingdom,
which he has promised to those who love
him? James 2:5

Dear Lord, You made all people equal,
no matter what they seem like on the
outside. Help me to see people the way
You see them and love them the way You
love them.

DAY 11

"Mr. Flacks, please come listen
to the evangelist speak."

Mr. Flacks was a wealthy clothing
manufacturer. What did he care about the
thirteen-year-old girl who sewed buttons on the
suitcoats he sold? He laughed at her request.

But the little girl tried again the next day
and the next and the next. Every day he
said no. Would you have given up?

On the last day the evangelist was speaking
in their city, the button girl burst into tears. "If
you don't trust in Jesus, you'll go to hell!"

Finally Mr. Flacks agreed to go hear
the evangelist and was saved. His life was
completely changed.

Years later he told his testimony in a
church. Because of his story, a young
woman named Margaret Nicholl decided
to become a missionary in Africa, where
many heard the gospel.

This happened because God used a little button girl whose name has been forgotten by people, but never by God. She was faithful.

***

His master said to him, "Well done, good and faithful servant. You have been faithful over a little; I will set you over much. Enter into the joy of your master." Matthew 25:21

Dear Lord, thank you for examples of people whose names aren't known who didn't give up telling others about You and living for You. Help me to be a person who doesn't give up.

DAY 12

Most of the tribal people of New Guinea were cannibals—when they killed an enemy in battle, they made his body into a sacrifice. They did terrible things to the person's body.

God has called you to be a living sacrifice, but that doesn't mean He wants you to give your body to let other people do bad things to you. It means He wants you to give your life for righteousness, for good things, not bad. It means offering your talents, skills, time, and life to help bring His gospel to others so they can rejoice in His love the way you do. The missionaries who went to the tribal people of New Guinea were examples of living sacrifices.

Being a living sacrifice is a good thing, offering our lives for the good work of the good news of God. It is a reason to rejoice, because the spiritual gifts He gives in return are always good ones!

***

I appeal to you therefore, brothers, by the
mercies of God, to present your bodies
as a living sacrifice, holy and acceptable
to God, which is your spiritual worship.
Romans 12:1

Dear God, help me to be a living sacrifice
so that am willing to work with joy for
Your Kingdom.

DAY 13

"All those Christians are filthy dogs." Hossein Soodmand was only seven years old, but he had learned his lesson well. Islam was the only true religion. He hated the Christians. In fact, he hated them so much that he decided to throw a stone to break that Christian woman's waterpot. But then when he tried to run away, he fell down and hurt himself badly. Instead of beating him, though, the Christian woman helped him up, tended his wound, and even gave him a piece of candy.

How could a Christian dog be so kind? Hossein didn't understand this woman's kindness, but he never forgot it.

It was many years before Hossein came to Christ, but that Christian woman was the first testimony to him of the love of Jesus.

Are you showing kindness, love, gentleness, and forgiveness to others? Even when you don't say a word about Jesus,

your life speaks as a testimony to those around you.

***

But I say to you who hear, Love your enemies, do good to those who hate you, bless those who curse you, pray for those who abuse you. Luke 6:27-28

Lord, help me to be like that woman and return kindness for hatred. Help me to be like Jesus, who loved even the ones who hurt Him.

DAY 14

Joy Ridderhof and the other missionaries were telling the people of Honduras how God's love was given freely through Jesus Christ. This made the priest furious! He hired someone to kill Joy, but God protected her.

Then the priest tried to kill Don Pedro, one of the new Christians. He pulled out a gun and aimed it at him. But someone grabbed the gun.

Then the priest tried to make Don Pedro bow down and worship a statue of Mary. He even whacked Don Pedro on the head with a crucifix!

This didn't help the priest have power over the people—it only made the people angry. The villagers were horrified at how evil he was, and many of them turned to the love of Christ that was shown through the missionaries.

It may seem like wicked people have all the power. But the power of the love of Jesus Christ will win in the end.

***

For the sake of Christ, then, I am content with weaknesses, insults, hardships, persecutions, and calamities. For when I am weak, then I am strong.
2 Corinthians 12:10

O Lord of hosts, No matter how much it looks like evil is winning now, You have already won the victory. Help me to remember that, even when things are hard.

One thing kept bothering young Amy Carmichael. She worried a lot about how she could live a holy life.

She knew it wasn't through works—she had learned that when she helped the old lady across the street. She knew her work with the shawlies wasn't going to make her holy. But what was the answer? She asked God to explain it to her.

When Amy was eighteen she went to a conference with a friend, praying that a speaker would help her understand. No one did, until the very last prayer. "O Lord," the speaker prayed, "we know that You are able to keep us from falling."

That's it! Amy thought. *The Lord is able to keep me from falling! My holiness doesn't depend on my work at all—it all depends on Him! All I have to do is trust!*

Amy's heart sang for joy. She understood that a life of holiness was lived by faith alone.

***

Now to him who is able to keep you from stumbling and to present you blameless before the presence of his glory with great joy, to the only God, our Savior, through Jesus Christ our Lord, be glory, majesty, dominion, and authority, before all time and now and forever. Amen. Jude 1:24-25

Lord Jesus, You are the only solution for a holy life. I need the holiness only You can give. Help me to put my faith in You moment by moment and day by day.

DAY 16

"It's a woman coming here? I thought it was going to be a man!"

Margaret Nicholl listened as the other missionaries discussed where in the world a new female missionary was going to stay. They finally decided to clean out the goat hut and let her sleep there.

What would you have thought of sleeping in a goat hut? But Margaret didn't say, "God's children should never sleep in goat huts." She accepted the offer cheerfully.

But the goats kept banging on the door, so she couldn't even sleep at night.

"We'll get a goat boy to take care of the goats and keep them away from your hut," the missionary leader promised.

The next day a ten-year-old African boy showed up at Margaret's door, smiling at her. That began a lifelong friendship

between Margaret and Kongi the goat boy. He taught her the tribal language, and she taught him about Jesus. Kongi became a missionary to his own people.

***

For my thoughts are not your thoughts, neither are your ways my ways, declares the LORD. For as the heavens are higher than the earth, so are my ways higher than your ways and my thoughts than your thoughts. Isaiah 55:8-9

Lord, thank You that You sometimes use hard things to bring about something beautiful. Help me to always be willing to cheerfully accept what You provide.

DAY 17

When the tribal people of New Guinea met the pale missionaries, they didn't think of them as real people. They called *themselves* the real people, and the missionaries were "tuans" or "respected strange ones."

When the missionaries preached the gospel, at first the tribal people couldn't believe it. After all, this good news was just for tuans, not for real people.

What would you do if you faced a situation like this?

But then . . . one of their own people came to preach the same good news to them! So the gospel wasn't just for tuans—it was for real people too!

It's important to always be open to the leading of the Holy Spirit when we're seeking to follow Him. It's also important to be humble—maybe someone else is

the one God wants to accomplish the work you've been trying to do! Ultimately, because He is the one who does it, all of us can rejoice.

***

I planted, Apollos watered, but God gave the growth. So neither he who plants nor he who waters is anything, but only God who gives the growth. 1 Corinthians 3:6-7

Thank You, Lord, that You use many different people to do Your work. Help me to be humble in doing Your work, willing to be a planter or a waterer, but expecting You to give the growth.

DAY 18

Many years ago in a small town in Australia, two women decided to start a Bible club to teach children about Jesus.

"Aunt Nell" and "Aunt Maggie" were never well known. But they were faithful to do what God had called them to do.

The two ladies knew that many of the children around them had never even heard about the Bible. They had never heard of Jesus except as a curse word. So they had good news to bring.

They would probably never have guessed that one shy teenage boy, who first heard the gospel from them, would one day take it to many in the faraway country of Ethiopia.

Have you ever thought about how the good news of salvation through Jesus Christ has been handed down from generation to generation? Somebody told somebody

who told somebody who told you. Thank God for faithful witnesses, both men and women, who have done that through the years!

***

And what you have heard from me in the presence of many witnesses entrust to faithful men [and women!] who will be able to teach others also. 2 Timothy 2:2

Thank You, Lord, for women who didn't need to be famous but just wanted to be faithful! Help me to be faithful too.

DAY 19

George Mueller was a pastor in England when he and his wife Mary decided to trust the Lord for everything they needed.

One day when they had only a few cents left and asked the Lord to provide for them, a lady gave them some money. Another day after they ate the last of their food, someone brought a loaf of bread and then another lady brought a whole dinner.

After a year of living this life of faith, George added up the value of everything he had received that year. He found the Lord had given them twice as much as the church would have given them for a salary!

The next Sunday morning he preached, "Do you think this way of living makes me worry? No! This way of living keeps me from worries. I'm strengthened in grace and filled with great joy. The way to have this kind of joy is to live this life of faith."

***

Trust in the Lord, and do good; so shalt thou dwell in the land, and verily thou shalt be fed. Psalm 37:3 KJV

Thank You, Lord, that You provide all that is needed for those who trust You by faith and seek You in prayer. Help me to always seek You.

DAY 20

Joy Ridderhof was very sick. She had to leave Honduras and go back home to California.

But even as she recovered and tried to trust and rejoice, the Lord began to bring some new thoughts to her mind.

"What if I could make recordings in Spanish that told the gospel?"

She thought about an old woman in Honduras who couldn't understand the gospel. *What if she had a record that could play the stories over and over?*

Even in a time of sickness, God was at work. While Joy rested and recovered, her mind was free to listen to what God wanted to show her. He was showing the next step in her work for Him.

Times of sickness can be discouraging. But even in them, God is working.

If your heart is turned to Him, He can show you something He wants to do in His plan.

***

For the Lord will not cast off forever, but, though he cause grief, he will have compassion according to the abundance of his steadfast love. Lamentations 3:31-32

Lord, You've shown that even in times of sickness and discouragement You still have a plan that You're carrying out. Help me to keep living in light of that wonderful truth.

DAY 21

While Joy recovered from her long illness, she learned to play the guitar. As soon as she was feeling better, someone let her use his recording studio to make one simple recording with some Spanish Bible verses, a short message, and some cheery gospel songs in Spanish.

Joy sent the record to her friends in Honduras. This was in 1936, over eighty years ago, when recordings were very new. The Honduran people had never before had recordings of the Christian message. The effect was electric! They were calling everyone to listen to it! Some who had never before been willing to listen to the gospel wanted to hear it when it was on a recording.

From a small seed of an idea, from one small effort to be faithful in what the Lord had called her to, Joy was reaching lives in another country, even while she was still in California. God was blessing her work.

***

And God is able to make all grace abound
to you, so that having all sufficiency in all
things at all times, you may abound in
every good work. 2 Corinthians 9:8

Thank You, Lord, that You are full of grace
and love giving it to Your people. I come to
You for that grace for today.

DAY 22

Amy Carmichael and some other missionaries boarded a ship that would sail for several weeks to get to Japan. Before long they found the ship was crawling with bugs. And worse, rats!

In England Amy had lived in an apartment where she couldn't get rid of the bugs and rats. So now on the ship, well, at least she was used to it! "We can give thanks even in this," she reminded the others. But the others didn't listen. They moaned and complained about the terrible problem.

"The Lord has sent us to this work," Amy said. "I'll give thanks and hope in Him."

Before the ship arrived in port, because of Amy's hope and courage in hardship, the captain came to trust in Christ.

You never know when other people are watching you and will be influenced by your words and actions. Keep following Jesus, even when things are hard.

***

You are the light of the world. A city set on a hill cannot be hidden. Nor do people light a lamp and put it under a basket, but on a stand, and it gives light to all in the house. In the same way, let your light shine before others, so that they may see your good works and give glory to your Father who is in heaven. Matthew 5:14-16

Dear Lord, You are the light in my soul. Help me to remember that people are watching me. Help them to see Christ in me.

DAY 23

The African sultan was so powerful he could command anything he wanted—except peace in his heart. One of the things he commanded was three hundred wives. They married him, and when he died, they were all buried alive with him in a gigantic grave.

The sultan's oldest son saw how angry his father had been, and how filled with torment. He knew his own mother had been buried alive.

One of the missionaries to the Central African Republic gave the gospel to this young man. Now the young sultan didn't have the same kind of power his father had, but he didn't want it. Instead, he had great happiness in Jesus, and power against the evil spirits who wanted to torment him.

When this Christian sultan died, his one wife dressed beautifully and welcomed people to his funeral. Together they rejoiced

that he was in heaven because of the saving power of Jesus Christ. What a difference the gospel makes!

***

And I will give you a new heart, and a new spirit I will put within you. And I will remove the heart of stone from your flesh and give you a heart of flesh. Ezekiel 36:26

Heavenly Father, thank You for the difference Your great salvation makes in people's lives. I pray that I'll see that difference in my own life more and more as I grow in You.

DAY 24

Anticipation is a wonderful feeling. Just imagine if a family member that you loved had gone far away and now you heard news that he or she is coming back tomorrow. Your anticipation would fill your whole body. You'd be eagerly looking forward to the coming of the one you love.

Almost all the Dani tribal group of New Guinea felt the same sense of anticipation. For so many years they had heard that someday *hai* would come—eternal life— and they didn't want to miss it when it came. They were so eagerly looking forward to it that when they heard the good news about the coming of Jesus Christ, many of them trusted in Him.

When the Bible uses the word *hope*, you can substitute the word *anticipation*. When God promises something, it's a sure thing. You can anticipate it with great expectation, knowing that God will accomplish His word.

***

Now hope that is seen is not hope. For who hopes for what he sees? But if we hope for what we do not see, we wait for it with patience. Romans 8:24-25

Thank You, Father, for Your promises that are sure! Increase my faith to believe You and expect You to fulfill the words You've promised.

DAY 25

One time Dick McLellan came back to his homeland of Australia from his mission work in Ethiopia. There he visited a small church where two young sisters asked him for his prayer card. They asked him to write on the back of the card six tribes to pray for.

Six years later Dick came back from Ethiopia again and visited the same small church. The girls said, "We've been praying for these tribes every night for the last six years."

"God has answered your prayers!" responded the missionary. "In the last six years, He has done great things in every one of those tribes!"

Keep praying for God to work in different people groups around the world—He delights to work through our prayers! Keep praying for Him to show Himself to be mighty

in the lives of the people you know. He is accomplishing His work, and He loves to do it through your prayers.

***

Finally, brothers, pray for us, that the word of the Lord may speed ahead and be honored, as happened among you.
2 Thessalonians 3:1

Lord God of hosts, I pray for the missionaries who are taking the gospel into the hard places, that those people will hear and believe. Help me to continue to pray faithfully for them.

DAY 26

In England in the 1800s, many children begged on the streets, children whose parents had died of diseases or other tragedies. George and Mary Mueller believed the Lord wanted them to provide food for those orphans. But how would Mary have enough food for the orphans George would bring back to the house? It seemed they wouldn't have enough.

But day after day God provided. One morning when George and his little daughter Lydia came back home with thirty-five orphans, Mary said, "George! While you were gone a man came to the door and brought porridge and molasses!" The orphans cheered—they would have a warm breakfast while Mr. Mueller told them about Jesus.

Are you able to trust God to do great things for you and through you? It doesn't happen all at once—it's a life of faith. Keep

trusting Him to do His work, to love you and love other people through you. See what He does!

***

I am the LORD thy God . . . open thy mouth wide, and I will fill it. Psalm 81:10 KJV

Lord, help me to trust You to love others through me. Make me a channel for Your love.

DAY 27

The people of the Japanese village had tied the man down onto boards and were putting burning coals on his body. "The fox spirit has control of him," they explained to Amy Carmichael, "but this fire will drive it out."

Amy was horrified. She said, "You can't cast this demon out, but it can be cast out by the power of the Lord Jesus Christ."

As soon as the possessed man heard the name of Jesus, he jumped and snarled and raged. If he hadn't been tied to the boards, he would have hurt Amy.

Amy and her Japanese Christian friend prayed and prayed. An hour later, the man was well, and the demons were gone. He said, "With all their many prayers to Buddha, the fox spirit inside me only laughed with scorn. But this Jesus God is powerful. Tell me more about Him." As Amy spoke to him about Jesus, he put all his faith in Him.

***

Be sober-minded; be watchful. Your
adversary the devil prowls around like a
roaring lion, seeking someone to devour.
1 Peter 5:8

O Lord, help me to be aware of the work
of the enemy of my soul and the way he
wants to attack me. Thank You for the
power You have against the evil one.

In Bible times, footwashing was the most disgusting job of all. When Jesus washed the disciples' feet, they were amazed He would do something so lowly. But He did it for love.

Margaret Nicholl did the same thing in Africa. When she met an orphan boy named Jiggerfoot, she brought him home and gladly crouched on the ground to clean his filthy, insect infested feet.

Would you have been willing to do something that lowly?

Margaret had to poke into Jiggerfoot's foot here and there, to get out those tiny terrible jiggers that had burrowed into his skin, and to clean out the infection.

Would you have been willing to do something that disgusting?

Margaret's work took many days. But as she worked, she told Jiggerfoot about Jesus

and His love. She also thought about how Jesus had washed the feet of the disciples. It was her joy to lovingly cleanse the feet of this African boy who needed the Savior.

***

Jesus, knowing that the Father had given all things into his hands, and that he had come from God and was going back to God, rose from supper. . . . Then he poured water into a basin and began to wash the disciples' feet. . . . John 13:3-5

Father in heaven, thank You for examples of people who are willing to do very lowly tasks to show Your love to others. Help me to be one of those people.

DAY 29

When Margaret Nicholl met Jiggerfoot, she saw that his feet were swollen with infection from the jiggers. Dozens of the tiny little bugs had burrowed into his skin.

Getting out the jiggers would be really painful. Margaret could have thought, "I don't want to hurt him more, so I won't take out those jiggers." But she knew that causing him pain was the only way to help him with the pain he already had.

Taking out the jiggers hurt—it hurt a lot. But when Margaret was finished, Jiggerfoot's feet were clean from all the bugs and all the infection. The pain was gone.

Sometimes the Lord needs to do a work in us that might hurt. But He does it because He loves us, to help us get rid of some "infection" in our souls, and to help build our faith and show us His great love. We can trust Him, that He's doing something for our good.

***

For the moment all discipline seems painful rather than pleasant, but later it yields the peaceful fruit of righteousness to those who have been trained by it. Hebrews 12:11

Dear Father, thank You that You love me enough to want to get the "jiggers" out of my life. Help me to remember when you discipline me that You do it because You love me.

"Where did these new women come from?" Margaret Nicholl wondered. She had never seen the four African women seated there ready for her Bible class. "How did you hear about our teaching?" she asked.

"Jiggerfoot!" one of them said. "He was always breaking our waterpots and stealing our food!"

Margaret's heart sank. He hadn't changed?

"But that was before," said another. "After he came here, he wanted us to forgive him, and he wanted to be our servant."

Another woman added, "So we fed him, and he told us the stories you told him while you were washing his feet."

"And now we're here," said the fourth. "We want to know this Jesus that can change somebody's life like He changed

Jiggerfoot's. Oh, he has a new name! Now he calls himself Jesus' Boy."

It was Margaret's delight to teach the women about the One who can make a thief into a joyful servant, who can make each person new.

***

Therefore, if anyone is in Christ, he is a new creation. The old has passed away; behold, the new has come. 2 Corinthians 5:17

Lord Jesus, thank You for the people whose lives have been changed by Your great salvation. I pray that I'll see that change in my own life more and more as I grow.

DAY 31

When the tribal people of New Guinea decided they wanted to follow the way of Christ, they burned their magic charms with huge bonfires. In one area, over 8,000 people gathered for the burning, throwing all their "power pieces" into the fire.

"We're rid of the old ways!" they cried. "We want forever life!"

But some of the witness men (or Christians) from other parts of the island said, "Burning your power pieces won't give you forever life. Only Jesus will give you that."

The same is true for you. Simply deciding to leave your old life isn't enough to be a real Christian. Just deciding to be good isn't enough to live the Christian life day by day. The Christian life is a life lived by daily faith in Christ and His transforming power, the same power that raised Him from the dead. He is the one that has the power not only to save you, but to change you.

***

Having the eyes of your hearts enlightened,
that you may know what is the hope to
which he has called you, what are the riches
of his glorious inheritance in the saints, and
what is the immeasurable greatness of his
power toward us who believe, according
to the working of his great might that he
worked in Christ when he raised him from the
dead and seated him at his right hand in the
heavenly places. Ephesians 1:18-20

O Lord, help me not to rely on keeping a list
of works or accomplishing certain things to
help me be a better Christian. Help me to live
by faith in Jesus Christ.

DAY 32

The Karen tribes of Southeast Asia had never seen a Bible but had many legends that might sound familiar. There was even a story of the first man and woman disobeying God by eating fruit!

One of their legends said a "brother" would come with good news from across the waters. They told that story generation after generation and never let go of hope. In fact, their legend even said they would be unable to sleep with anticipation for what that brother would bring.

Finally in the 1800s George and Sarah Boardman came. The "white book", which the legends said had been lost so long ago, had returned, telling how to reach the great God through Jesus Christ.

Except for these legends, the Karen people had lived dark and hopeless lives. To hear the good news of the gospel filled them

with hope that now they could truly have a relationship with the true God, through His Son, Jesus Christ.

***

Let the nations be glad and sing for joy, for you judge the peoples with equity and guide the nations upon earth. Psalm 67:4

Thank You, Lord, that you prepare people's hearts even through strange legends to receive Your word! Thank you that Your word goes out over all the world through Your faithful servants, and that the nations can sing for joy because of Your salvation.

In 1935, the people of Colombia feared the Bible. When missionaries John and Rachel Harbeson and Jack Thomas tried to give away Bibles, the people mocked them and called them names. They even threw rotten fruit and beat them.

Then the missionaries started giving the Bibles away secretly. It turned out there were a few Colombians who were hungry for God's Word, but they were afraid to show their interest in public.

The missionaries knew that being cursed and beaten was just something to be expected—Jesus said so. But in every place, God has His people, and they wanted to find them. Getting beaten was worth it. It was worth it to find the people who really did want the Word of God.

When people don't believe the gospel, we don't need to be discouraged. In every place, God has His people, and He

has called us to tell others, with love and kindness, no matter the cost.

***

Blessed are you when others revile you and persecute you and utter all kinds of evil against you falsely on my account. Rejoice and be glad, for your reward is great in heaven, for so they persecuted the prophets who were before you.
Matthew 5:11-12

Thank You, Lord, that You have Your people in every place, and we can trust that You are calling them. Help me to be a faithful servant for You.

DAY 34

After three years, Joy Ridderhof recovered from her long illness and planned to return to Honduras where she had been a missionary.

But she had also been making Spanish gospel recordings. Not just one, but now almost fifty! She sent them out to many Spanish speaking countries. Then someone asked her to make a recording in another language.

Joy didn't want to! "I must go to the Spanish-speaking people, Lord," she said. But the Lord reminded her that He had others to reach too.

Finally she said, "Yes, Lord. I'll make recordings in as many languages as You want me to." It was a hard decision, but Joy felt peace. Little did she know it was a step on the road to a worldwide ministry.

The Lord rarely shows His people His plan for them all at once. It's step by step as we surrender to Him and say, "Yes, Lord." He can be trusted as we follow Him.

***

Therefore, as you received Christ Jesus the Lord, so walk in him, rooted and built up in him and established in the faith, just as you were taught, abounding in thanksgiving.
Colossians 2:6-7

You have a perfect plan for my life, Lord, even when I can't see it at all. Help me to walk in faith that You will show it to me, step by step.

DAY 35

One time young Fanny Crosby picked one of Mrs. Hawley's prize roses just because she loved the soft feel and the beautiful smell. When Mrs. Hawley asked Fanny about that rose, Fanny lied and said she didn't know anything.

Mrs. Hawley got out her Bible and read the story of Ananias and Sapphira. "They both lied to the Holy Spirit," she said, "so the Lord struck them both dead." Then Mrs. Hawley left the room.

Fanny sighed. Finally she went to Mrs. Hawley. "I didn't tell the truth before," she said. "I really did pick that rose."

When you do wrong, you may try to quiet your conscience by telling yourself you really didn't do anything wrong, or it's not a big deal, or it's not anybody else's business to know. But listen to the voice of the Holy

Spirit and be truthful. God is pleased when His faithful children deal truthfully.

**

Lying lips are an abomination to the LORD, but those who act faithfully are his delight.
Proverbs 12:22

Lord, I know you hate lying lips and love the truth. Help me to always deal honestly and truthfully, like a true child of God.

Amy Carmichael believed she should pray to know the will of God in a certain situation, and then pray in faith that this will of His would be done. In Japan God put this faith to the test.

When Amy prepared to go speak to the people in a village, she asked the Lord what His will was for that village. One time she was sure the Lord was saying He wanted to save four people.

"Four people?" the other missionaries cried. "Most missionaries in Japan see only four souls saved in a whole year! How can you ask for four souls in one day?"

But Amy insisted this was what she believed the Lord wanted her to pray for. She prayed, her friend prayed, and even some of the other missionaries prayed.

That day, in that village, four people trusted Christ. This may not sound like a lot to

you, but to the missionaries in Japan, it was miraculous.

***

Now faith is the assurance of things hoped for, the conviction of things not seen.
Hebrews 11:1

Lord, help me to seek Your will and then walk in it by faith, the way Amy Carmichael did.

"Cannibals!" Margaret Nicholl Laird cried out to her husband Guy. "We won't be safe among cannibals!"

"If God wants us there, He'll take care of us," Guy reminded her. He bought a large herd of goats to provide milk for their three children. Kongi the goat boy began to lead the herd of goats to the new location.

"Won't Kongi steal the goats?" someone asked.

"No," said Margaret. "I can trust him to keep them safe."

You can trust Me too, the Lord reminded Margaret. *I will keep you safe.*

The Lairds drove in the truck to the new mission station. Kongi wasn't there yet, but Margaret knew she could trust him.

The little cannibals peered at the strange white people and laughed with delight at

the baby. These people didn't seem fierce at all—they seemed like children.

Then Kongi arrived with all the goats. He was trustworthy. *You're trustworthy too, Lord,* Margaret thought. *You will keep us safe.*

***

But let all who take refuge in you rejoice; let them ever sing for joy, and spread your protection over them, that those who love your name may exult in you. Psalm 5:11

Thank You, Lord, for Your loving protection. Help me to live each day in light of Your faithfulness and protection.

DAY 38

Dave Scovill hadn't known the Dani language for very long. But his friend, a Dani boy named Wat, told him to tell a Bible story to the thousand people who had come to listen.

Dave spoke slowly: "Jesus told a story about a man who planted good seed. But his enemy planted weeds. The man let the grain and the weeds grow together until the harvest. Then he burned the weeds. Jesus' followers asked what the story meant. Jesus said:

The one who sows the good seed is the Son of Man. The field is the world, and the good seed is the sons of the kingdom. The weeds are the sons of the evil one, and the enemy who sowed them is the devil. At the end of the world, the good seed will be gathered and the weeds will be burned.

Matthew 13:37-39

The Dani people were fascinated by this story and began memorizing the words Dave

spoke. Wat said, "Tonight around the fire, they won't talk about war and spirits the way they usually do. They'll talk about that story."

As the people discussed the story and asked Dave questions, many of them came to understand how important it was to be part of the "good seed" of Jesus. Is that true of you?

***

Dear God, thank You for the parables of Jesus that show us Your truth. Help me by faith to be one of the "good seed" who brings forth fruit for Your kingdom.

DAY 39

In Iran in the 1980s, the Bible was illegal. When Mina found a Persian New Testament on the library floor, she had never seen one before. Mina knew it was a holy book, so she was excited to show her family.

But her father yelled at her. "We respect that book, but don't ever touch it again!" he said.

Mina was shocked. What could be so bad about a holy book? She decided to read it secretly.

This Jesus—He was so different from Mohammed! He treated women with respect, He didn't rob, He spoke with wisdom and kindness. Mina wanted to understand more. How could she?

You have the New Testament too. You can also read about Jesus and see his wisdom and kindness. Even if you've known

the stories of Jesus for many years, you can ask God to help you see them with new eyes, like Mina's. And you can ask Him to help you understand.

***

Many who heard him were astonished, saying, "Where did this man get these things? What is the wisdom given to him? How are such mighty works done by his hands?" Mark 6:2

Thank You, Lord Jesus, for the mighty works and the wonderful teachings and the great salvation I can learn about in Your Word. Help me to appreciate it and never take it for granted.

DAY 40

Mina read in the New Testament that Jesus talked about giving rest to the burdened. Was He talking about the burdens of religion?

Mina had tried so hard to please Allah, to keep all the many, many rules of Islam. "I've tried to please you for so long," she prayed, "but I'm exhausted. Please, if you care, show me."

That night Mina dreamed that a voice called, "I am the way, the truth, and the life! No one comes to the Father except through me!"

Mina sat up in bed, shocked. Who was that? Somehow she knew if she could just find a Christian, she would find out the answers to her questions.

Have you felt like you have to keep a lot of rules to please God? That's not Christianity.

If you are truly in Christ, God is pleased with you. He is working His good work in You by faith. This is a reason to rejoice!

***

Come to me, all who labor and are heavy laden, and I will give you rest.
Matthew 11:28

Lord Jesus, thank You that You've done all the work for me. Help me to keep looking to You by faith to do Your work in me.

DAY 41

By 1943 Joy Ridderhof and her friend Ann had recorded the gospel in many languages. Then they went to Mexico, where the Lord brought them to thirty-three tribes who didn't have a Bible in their own language and had never heard the gospel before.

When one tribal person who could speak some Spanish helped them make a recording, it was a wonderful moment. The man stood in awe as he listened to his own voice telling words in his own language about the true God and His Son, Jesus Christ.

Joy clapped her hands. "This," she said. "This is what God made me for!"

Sometimes we may think God has one plan for our lives—Joy thought she was supposed to be a missionary in Honduras. But then we can find that God's plan goes in a different direction. As long as we're following Him, we can trust, and we can rejoice.

***

I know, O LORD, that the way of man is not in himself, that it is not in man who walks to direct his steps. Jeremiah 10:23

O Lord, I worship You as the one who has made good plans for Your people, even when we don't expect it. Help me to live in light of Your good plans.

DAY 42

Joy and Ann decided to drive from Mexico a thousand more miles to visit the Christians in Honduras where Joy had been a missionary. How glad they were to see her! "We love the Spanish gospel recordings you made!" they said.

Joy told them what God had been doing through her new ministry, Gospel Recordings. "God has called me to other people groups.

"He reminded me of John 10:16, where Jesus said:

"'And I have other sheep that are not of this fold. I must bring them also, and they will listen to my voice. So there will be one flock, one shepherd.'"

The Christians of Marcala felt sad and happy at the same time. They wouldn't see her again, but were happy that she was bringing the gospel to people around the

world. "Some of us came to Christ through your gospel recordings," they said. "We're glad for this good work."

Sometimes it's hard saying goodbye to someone we love who is taking the gospel to another part of the world. But we can remember that the Lord wants to call people from all over to rejoice in His great salvation.

***

Lord Jesus, my Good Shepherd, You have sheep all over the world that You want to bring into Your fold. Thank You that You are using faithful people to do that.

DAY 43

When Fanny Crosby was still young, she found out her grandma was about to die. She hugged her grandma and cried. Grandma asked, "Will you meet me one day in our Father's house on high?"

Fanny didn't know the answer. She didn't know if she was in God's kingdom or not. But finally she said, "By the grace of God, I will."

Before she died, Grandma prayed with Fanny that God would bring her safely into His kingdom. Fanny never forgot her question.

God wants you in His kingdom too. If you haven't ever trusted in Jesus Christ, you can trust in Him now to bring you out of the kingdom of darkness into His kingdom. Give Him your life, and trust Him with your future. Do you think it means you won't be able to do what you want? No, instead, it means you'll be able to see clearly, to want the things that are good.

***

He has delivered us from the domain of darkness and transferred us to the kingdom of his beloved Son. Colossians 1:13

Father, help me to be a true child of God, trusting in Jesus Christ and His sacrifice for me. Bring me into His kingdom, I pray.

DAY 44

As a young missionary in India, Amy Carmichael heard a saying, "Say money, and a corpse will open its mouth." Some missionaries told her that even Christian Indians insisted on being paid more than they were worth to do any work.

"How can this be?" thought Amy. "Why don't Christians want to work without pay? The Lord's work is so much more important!" Then she prayed, "Lord, give me workers who are willing to work for You without pay."

The Lord answered that prayer. Amy was able to work with a group of Indian Christian women who called themselves the Starry Cluster. "We want to do the Lord's work without pay," they said. "The Lord's work is far too important."

What is your attitude about being paid for your work for the Lord? Are you willing to work for Him without pay, trusting Him

to provide what you need? He is a faithful God, and will do it.

***

But Peter said, "I have no silver and gold, but what I do have I give to you. In the name of Jesus Christ of Nazareth, rise up and walk!" Acts 3:6

Thank You, Lord Jesus, that You give good gifts that are far better than money! Help me to learn to live for those good gifts in You.

DAY 45

Indian woman wore thousands of dollars' worth of jewels, even if they didn't have enough money to feed their families. Removing their jewels was unthinkable.

But the Starry Cluster decided they would sell their jewels and use the money for the advance of the gospel. In India, this was radical Christianity, a huge sacrifice. The Christian Indian women expected other Indians to be angry, but they didn't expect anger from the Indians who were *Christians*!

Actually the Hindus admired them. "If you give up your jewels for your religion, it must be a true religion indeed," they said. The Starry Cluster's radical sacrifice gave them more opportunities to give the gospel to others.

Is God calling you to radical sacrifice?

The Starry Cluster discovered an extra advantage they hadn't thought about.

Now that they didn't have any jewels, all those dozens of robbers along the roads weren't interested in attacking them. They could even be safe traveling at night!

***

For whoever would save his life will lose it, but whoever loses his life for my sake will find it. For what will it profit a man if he gains the whole world and forfeits his soul? Or what shall a man give in return for his soul? Matthew 16:25-26

Lord help me to remember what is truly important. Help me to be willing to give up earthly riches for the riches You offer.

DAY 46

Chief Yetaman lay in a hut, dying. Two of his seventy wives stood over him, using leaves to wipe the pus out of his infected wound.

When Margaret Laird examined his wound, she said, "I have medicine for infections! I can help you!"

Every morning for a month, Margaret prepared an antiseptic solution. Then she traveled from her little hut to the far-off village of Chief Yetaman to gently run the solution through his infected wound. Every evening she did the same thing.

After a month, there was Chief Yetaman at her door, healed! He brought many gifts, but Mr. Laird said, "The main gift we want is for all your people to listen to the words I have to tell."

Chief Yetaman sent messages through all the villages for the people to listen to

what the missionaries had to say. Many of the people all around came to listen and were saved.

***

And great crowds came to him, bringing with them the lame, the blind, the crippled, the mute, and many others, and they put them at his feet, and he healed them, so that the crowd wondered, when they saw the mute speaking, the crippled healthy, the lame walking, and the blind seeing. And they glorified the God of Israel. Matthew 15:30-31

Thank You, Lord, that You heal people for Your glory. Thank You that when You heal people, Your Word can go forth with power.

When Margaret Laird was helping Chief Yetaman get well from his infection, she had to spend a lot of time preparing the antiseptic solution.

Then she climbed into a contraption called a push-push for a very uncomfortable ride, as two small African men pushed her for forty-five minutes to get to the chief's village. Then she spent time taking care of the chief. Then the small men pushed her forty-five minutes back home.

And that was all just in the morning! In the evening, they did it all again. Every day for a month.

Why did Margaret spend so much time helping a man she didn't even know? She did it for love, because she wanted the African people to know the Savior, Jesus Christ. When Chief Yetaman wanted

his people to hear the gospel, Margaret rejoiced. Her hope was that many would come to know the great Savior who loved them so.

**

I will most gladly spend and be spent for your souls. 2 Corinthians 12:15

Dear Lord, thank You for the people who are willing to "spend and be spent" to show Your love to others. Help me to be willing to give my energies, my abilities, and my life to see Your love and Your glory spread abroad.

DAY 48

When Elinor Young was four she developed polio, a terrible crippling disease. After being sick for a long time, she still had to wear braces on her legs just to be able to walk with crutches. Even so, when Elinor was nine, she was sure God was calling her to be a missionary.

"You must be misunderstanding God's call," said some people. How could she become a missionary when she was a cripple?

But she did, and in some of the highest mountain areas in the world! The tribal people of Papua, Indonesia, loved her and carried her around on a mountain chair so she could give the gospel to many.

Has God called you to do something that some people think is impossible? If He has called you to a work, you can be sure He will accomplish it. It may take a long time, but you can trust Him that He will do it.

***

He who calls you is faithful; he will surely do it. 1 Thessalonians 5:24

Lord, I trust You that for every work You have called me to do, You will accomplish that good work in me.

Some women who worked in a cathedral in Colombia secretly listened to the missionaries preach. For a whole year they listened, hardly able to believe that such good news was really true. Then, because they were listening to the teachings from the Bible, the priest told them they were going to hell. The priests wanted to control people's lives, and they knew the good news of the gospel would set people free.

To most Colombians, a priest's curse seemed like the worst thing in the world. The sisters started to cry. But the missionaries said, "Don't cry, because your salvation doesn't depend on them, but on Christ."

One of the sisters said, "Do you think I'm weeping for us? No! I'm weeping for those wicked priests!"

Your salvation doesn't depend on any good things you can do or what other

people say about you. Your salvation comes only through faith in the work that Christ has already done.

***

For freedom Christ has set us free; stand firm therefore, and do not submit again to a yoke of slavery. Galatians 5:1

Thank You, Lord Jesus, that our salvation depends not on what we can do, but on what You have already done! Thank You!

DAY 50

Joy Ridderhof's mission was recording the gospel in thousands of tribal languages so people groups could hear the good news of Jesus Christ. Her helpers translated from English . . . to the country's main language . . . to the tribal language. Then the native speaker spoke the words into a microphone.

But in an Ethiopian hospital, one young man spoke a language so foreign that nobody had heard it before. No one could translate.

But the one person who knew the mysterious tribal language happened to get a toothache . . . and happened to come to that hospital . . . and happened to be put in the bed right next to that young man. He translated, the language was recorded, and the young man came to Christ.

It was many years before the young man's people group was found, but that's another story!

God loves to use surprising coincidences to bring glory to His great Name.

***

Nations will fear the name of the Lord, and all the kings of the earth will fear your glory.
Psalm 102:15

Thank You, Lord, that You care about small details in bringing the gospel to the nations. Thank You for Your faithfulness.

DAY 51

After years of ministry and trusting God, George and Mary Mueller were able to build large orphan houses for many orphans. Many visitors came to see the work they were doing to help the orphans of England.

One day the visitors who came to the orphan house were a young couple getting ready to be missionaries. It was Hudson and Maria Taylor, soon to leave for China. They marveled at all the Lord had done when the Muellers had asked no one for money except God Himself. George Mueller talked and prayed with them, and they went on their way.

Hudson was a young man who wanted to follow George Mueller's excellent example of living by faith. When the Taylors went off to China, Hudson started a mission organization, the China Inland Mission, where every missionary lived by faith, never

asking for money and simply trusting God just like George Mueller. As Hudson grew older, others looked to him as an example too.

***

One generation shall commend your works to another, and shall declare your mighty acts. Psalm 145:4

Dear God, help me to follow the examples of trusting You of faithful men and women who have gone before me. Help me to be a good example of trusting You to the people who will come behind me.

Fanny Crosby was able to go to a school for the blind. There she was able to learn to read Braille, but she also learned simply by listening to the teachers read the textbooks.

At the blind school, Fanny discovered her talent for writing poetry. She could write many poems a day, both serious and funny. The other students loved her writing.

One day the principal called her into his office. "Miss Crosby," he said, "I've seen you're becoming very proud of your accomplishments. I want to warn you not to depend on the praise of men. The talents you have belong to God—give Him the credit for all you do."

How would you have felt if someone had spoken to you that way about your best talents and abilities? Do you want to

claim them as your own, or do you want to acknowledge that they came from God?

Fanny was grateful for the principal's wise words.

***

[Jesus said,] "How can you believe, when you receive glory from one another and do not seek the glory that comes from the only God?" John 5:44

Dear Father, I know You've given me talents to use for You. Help me to not want to glory in them myself but to use them for Your glory.

Amy Carmichael's friend Ponnammal explained to her about how Indian women thought. Indian women had small worlds, she said, because they lived small lives. They were told that they couldn't think about any life beyond their own children and their own village. To them, religion was only for men.

But Jesus reached down to open the minds and hearts of some of these women who couldn't see beyond their own village. Some of them came to Christ and became the Starry Cluster, traveling with Amy to give the good news to others.

Have you ever thought about the fact that you can be so distracted by the things of this world—entertainment, fantasy, social media—that you end up living a small life? Your life may seem big, but it will really be small if you don't see the things

that are eternal. When you live your life for Jesus Christ, you're living the biggest, most significant life of all.

***

If then you have been raised with Christ, seek the things that are above, where Christ is seated at the right hand of God. Set your minds on things that are above, not on things that are on earth.
Colossians 3:1-2

Father, thank You that the "things above" are the true treasures. Help me not to be distracted by the things that won't last.

Margaret Laird had moved into cannibal country with her family. But now she found out that an elegant African lady was coming to visit her. "What will I do?" she thought. "I don't have anything in my hut that's at all elegant! I don't know what I'll feed her! I don't know what she'll think of me!"

Margaret was suffering from a different kind of "fear of man." She wasn't afraid of the cannibals, but she was afraid of someone looking down on her.

Have you ever experienced that kind of "fear of man"—worrying about what someone will think of you?

God used the visit from the elegant lady to help Margaret overcome her "fear of man." When Madame Eboue came to visit, there were suddenly so many emergencies, so many people needing help, that Margaret didn't have any time at all to worry

about impressing her. Instead, God showed Margaret that He was sufficient even in that experience.

***

For I, the Lᴏʀᴅ your God, hold your right hand; it is I who say to you, "Fear not, I am the one who helps you." Isaiah 41:13

Dear Lord, help me to remember not to be worried about what other people will think of me, but just to trust You and live for You. Thank You for Your love!

"The doctor told my parents I might die." Elinor Young spoke to some boys from the Kimyal tribe in Papua, Indonesia, explaining the polio that had left her legs so weak.

"But you didn't die," said a boy. "God wanted you here to help bring us the good news in our language."

Later the elders of the tribe gave her a special name: "Bad Legs." *What a strange name!* Elinor thought. When she asked why, Siud explained. "All the Christians who brought God's Word to us have left, even though they have good legs. But you've come from your far land to tell us about Jesus, even with your bad legs. You're small and weak, but you've stayed to help us understand God's Word. Your bad legs are a gift from God to us."

Who would have thought bad legs could be a gift from God? But to the Kimyals, Elinor's bad legs showed them how great God's love was for them.

***

And I was with you in weakness and in fear and much trembling, and my speech and my message were not in plausible words of wisdom, but in demonstration of the Spirit and of power, so that your faith might not rest in the wisdom of men but in the power of God. 1 Corinthians 2:3-5

Dear Lord, I see from the example of Elinor Young that even what seems to be my worst handicap can be the thing that brings You the most glory. Help me to remember that and trust You in it.

"I need to find a follower of Jesus to help me understand," Mina thought. "How can I find one?" In the Muslim country of Iran, it seemed impossible!

Mina's cousins, very strict Muslims, visited. Mina invited her sweet cousin Monir into her bedroom to talk, but then gasped when she saw she had forgotten to hide her New Testament. Would Monir tell on her?

But Monir grabbed the book. "I'm a secret follower of Jesus!" she cried. "He's alive! He is the way, the truth, and the life! Mina, keep reading this book, and keep asking Him to show Himself to you. He will!"

God answered Mina's prayer to find a follower of Jesus to help her understand more about Christianity and lead her in the right way. He'll answer your prayers for the same.

Jesus is the way, the truth, and the life. Keep reading the Bible, and keep asking Him to show Himself to you. And He will!

***

Jesus said to him, "I am the way, and the truth, and the life. No one comes to the Father except through me." John 14:6

Thank You, Lord Jesus, that You are the only Way, the only Truth, and the only Life. Help me to know You better.

DAY 57

In a secret meeting of Christians, the Lord Jesus showed Himself to Mina. "I want to belong to Jesus Christ!" she cried out.

Pastor Hossein Soodmand asked her to pray, "Lord Jesus, Savior of the world, I believe You died on the cross for me and God raised You from death. I confess and repent of my sins. I turn from all false prophets and other religions. I believe on You as my Savior and Lord."

In Iran, Christians could be killed for their faith. But it was worth it. Mina was filled with the light and love and power of Christ. She had been seeking the presence of God, and now she had it.

Have you fully believed on Jesus Christ as your Savior and Lord, not just in your head, but in your heart? Have you confessed and repented of your sins? Have you turned from all other beliefs? It's not too late. Today can be that day.

***

. . . We appeal to you not to receive the grace of God in vain. For he says, "In a favorable time I listened to you, and in a day of salvation I have helped you." Behold, now is the favorable time; behold, now is the day of salvation.
2 Corinthians 6:1-2

Lord Jesus, help me to trust You for my full salvation, not just in my head, but in my heart. Help me to turn from other ways of thinking and turn fully to You.

DAY 58

In a village of Southeast Asia, the people were wailing, filled with hopeless despair. Someone had died, and there was no hope.

But there were a few Christians who had gathered to hear the missionary George Boardman speak from I Corinthians 15:42-44. While the hopeless wailing went on outside, he spoke of the hope we have in Jesus Christ.

What is sown is perishable; what is raised is imperishable. It is sown in dishonor; it is raised in glory. It is sown in weakness; it is raised in power. It is sown a natural body; it is raised a spiritual body. 1 Corinthians 15:42-44

What does this mean? It means that we need to have no fear of death, no hopeless despair when someone who loves Jesus has died. The body will go into the ground, but the spirit will live forever, in glory and power, with Him. This is a reason for great hope, even when we grieve the loss of someone we love.

We know the things we can't see are more real than the things we can see. We know if we trust Him, we can live forever with Him.

***

Thank You, Father, that I can trust You in life or death! Thank You that as a believer in Jesus Christ, I don't need to feel hopeless despair when someone who loves You has died.

Not long after George Boardman preached at the funeral where the Christians trusted in Jesus Christ, he himself became very sick. But even though he was so sick, he insisted on going to the baptism of several dozen of the people of the Karen tribe. After the baptism, and before they could get home, George was dead.

Sarah, George's wife, felt deep grief and sorrow. But even in the blackness of her grief, she trusted the Lord.

How is someone able to rest in God's will like that? Sarah had come to know who God really was, through His Word, and through her own experience in her life. She knew He was still a good and loving and faithful God.

Sarah stayed in the tribal area and continued to teach the villagers about Jesus. Three years later, Adoniram Judson, also a missionary to Southeast Asia, asked her to marry him. Even in this, God was faithful.

***

As it is my eager expectation and hope that I will not be at all ashamed, but that with full courage now as always Christ will be honored in my body, whether by life or by death. For to me to live is Christ, and to die is gain. Philippians 1:20-21

Heavenly Father, I want to trust You that You will do right in my life and in the lives of those I love, whether it is by life or by death.

DAY 60

When their father got leprosy, Jose and Carlos had to go live in the Colombian leprosy colony with him. There they heard the true gospel and were saved. When they came to visit their cousins at Marco Franco's house, they gave the gospel in a way that the Franco family would accept: through the Christmas story.

The Franco family thought of themselves as good Catholics, but they had never even seen a Bible.

"When the angels told the shepherds they had *good news*," Jose said, "that was the same word as *gospel*." Then Jose and Carlos told the family that all who believe in Jesus Christ can receive salvation. "All who trust Him will rise from the dead with Him."

"What!" This news seemed too good to be true. Believing it meant they would be *evangelicos* instead of Catholics. There

would be a price to pay in persecution. Would salvation in Jesus Christ be worth the price?

***

For I am not ashamed of the gospel, for it is the power of God for salvation to everyone who believes, to the Jew first and also to the Greek. Romans 1:16

Dear God, thank You that salvation in Jesus Christ, is worth the price of persecution. Help me to take hold of that truth more deeply and understand it more fully. Thank You that You are providing salvation for people all over the world.

Rosa was the Franco children's mother. Rosa had made a vow to the El Cristo Rey Christ statue to keep giving offerings to it if it would heal her son's foot. But when Carlos and Jose told the gospel about the *living* Christ, she stopped. She knew the statue was nothing but cold, dead metal.

Then Rosa prayed to the living Christ that if He would heal her son's foot, she would become an *evangelico*. As she continued to pray, she saw that her son's foot was healed. He had done it!

Rosa honored her vow to the living Christ. The next time Jose and Carlos visited, she was ready to proclaim her faith in the true and living Lord Jesus.

At first Marco was furious! But in time he began to believe as well. Rosa and Marco and all their children trusted in Jesus, even

through intense persecution. It was worth it to have a God who was alive and loved them.

***

Their idols are silver and gold, the work of human hands. They have mouths, but do not speak; eyes, but do not see. They have ears, but do not hear; noses, but do not smell. They have hands, but do not feel; feet, but do not walk; and they do not make a sound in their throat. Those who make them become like them; so do all who trust in them. Psalm 115:4-8

Lord Jesus Christ, thank You that You are the living God who hears me and loves me. Show me Yourself more and more as I trust You.

DAY 62

Joy Ridderhof's work, Gospel Recordings, grew and grew. Now in 1947 she had many volunteers working for her. But there was so much work to do— writing letters, planning recordings, making the recordings, copying records, shipping them out—it seemed they would never get it all done. They were exhausted and stressed.

"We need to pray more," Joy said.

"But we already pray together every morning," said one volunteer.

"We need to start taking off an entire day every week for prayer," Joy answered.

The team was astonished. "We already can't do everything we need to do. Now we *really* won't be able to!"

But they spent every Wednesday in prayer and praise. After one year they found that they had gotten more done than ever. And they had done it without worrying!

They learned the truth that trusting, praying, and rejoicing allows God to do much more work through us.

***

Trust in the LORD with all your heart, and do not lean on your own understanding. In all your ways acknowledge him, and he will make straight your paths. Proverbs 3:5-6

Lord, You love to work on behalf of Your people when they come to You in prayer. Help me to remember to do that, the way Joy Ridderhof and her team did.

DAY 63

When she was a student and a teacher at the School for the Blind, Fanny Crosby became famous for her poetry. Famous people came to visit her—and not just any famous people. Presidents of the United States came! Fanny was well-known and well-loved by many.

Fanny's mother was also well-pleased with her daughter's accomplishments. But one day when Fanny was visiting, she asked, "Is the Lord Jesus in your life, Fanny?"

Fanny laughed and blushed. How was she to answer that? Her life was full of her own activities and accomplishments. There didn't seem to be room for Jesus.

Have you ever felt that way? Like there isn't room for Jesus in your full and busy life? You can ask Him to do something to get your attention, to turn your eyes away from the

things of this world, with all its distractions. These things won't last. Ask God to help you focus on the spiritual world that you can't see. These things are eternal.

***

As we look not to the things that are seen but to the things that are unseen. For the things that are seen are transient, but the things that are unseen are eternal.
2 Corinthians 4:18

Father in heaven, I know that the things I can see will fade away and the spiritual things I can't see will last forever. Help me to value the things I can't see more than the things I can see.

DAY 64

A girl named Arulai believed there must be one God greater than all the other Hindu gods, so she began to pray to know Him. One day she heard some strangers in her village talking about "the living God," so she knew all the Hindu gods must be dead ones. The next day the strangers spoke of this living God and said His name was "Jesus"..

Arulai knew so little, but she kept praying to this "living God" named "Jesus", asking Him to help her understand more about Him. He answered prayers to show her He was real.

"That foreign woman right there," she prayed, "I want to go to her and learn more about the living God." And God brought Arulai to Amy Carmichael.

Do you want to know the true God, the real God? Keep praying and asking Him to

show Himself to you. Don't give up. Keep asking. He is faithful, and will do it.

***

You have said, "Seek my face." My heart says to you, "Your face, Lᴏʀᴅ, do I seek."
Psalm 27:8

O Lord, help me to continue seeking You. Please show Yourself to me.

One day Arulai's father came to get her from the village where she was learning about Jesus. He wanted to take her back where she would be forced again into the Hindu world. Arulai cried out to God, and He gave her a promise from His Word that He would keep her safe.

With great peace Arulai faced her father. "My God has promised me He'll bring me back here no matter what," she announced joyfully.

Arulai's father was stunned. When he reached out to grab her, his arm fell limp at his side. "I can't do anything against your powerful God!" he said. "I won't force you to go with me. I fear your supreme God." He left Arulai with Amy, where she stayed for many years telling people about the Living God.

God is faithful. If your heart is to love and serve Him, He will protect you as long as He has work for you to do.

***

The LORD is my light and my salvation; whom shall I fear? The LORD is the stronghold of my life; of whom shall I be afraid? Psalm 27:1

God, help me to keep trusting You even when things happen that make me afraid. Strengthen my trust in You, I pray.

Kongi the goat boy was twenty-six years old now. He had studied at Bible school and prepared to teach his people. But leprosy had eaten away some of his toes and was spreading over his body.

Sometimes life is very hard.

Mama Laird had tried to help him, but it wasn't working. "You need to go to the leprosy colony at Sibut," she said. "They have better medicine and can help you more than I can."

"You're trying to get rid of me," Kongi said bitterly. "Mama loves her goat boy when he's well, but not when he's sick."

Sometimes life looks almost hopeless.

"I love you no less now," Mama said. "But the Lord may have a mighty work for you even in the leprosy colony. There is still hope."

Kongi didn't even raise his eyes to say goodbye to Mama as he left on the back of a truck. "Lord, help him to know Your hope," Mama prayed.

***

Why are you cast down, O my soul, and why are you in turmoil within me? Hope in God; for I shall again praise him, my salvation and my God. Psalm 42:11

Lord, sometimes life is so hard. Sometimes it's hard to trust You. Help me to hope when life is dark.

DAY 67

When Mama Laird was finally able to visit the leprosy colony many months later, she heard laughter from one of the huts. Inside she saw many people gathered, laughing. One of them was Kongi!

"Kongi, you're so different!" she exclaimed.

"Mama, you told me that God might have a great work for me in the leprosy colony. You were right! Please come meet all my friends."

Kongi had felt despair, but he trusted Jesus and found hope. Then he offered hope to the other people around him. Mama could see that many had come to Jesus through his fervent witness in the leprosy colony. Even the doctor at the colony trusted in Christ.

Eventually, Kongi's leprosy was healed, but he stayed at the colony for twenty more years, continuing to preach and teach,

telling others about the hope they can find in Jesus Christ.

As one who had gone from despair to hope, he knew what he was talking about.

***

Remember your word to your servant, in which you have made me hope. This is my comfort in my affliction, that your promise gives me life. Psalm 119:49-50

Dear God, thank You that You restore hope to those who experience despair. Please help people I know who are experiencing despair, and restore hope to them.

DAY 68

How could it be? How could God want this to happen? After eighteen years with the Kimyal tribe, in 1991 Elinor Young had to leave. The polio that had afflicted her as a child had left its mark. Now her muscles felt so weak, and she felt tired all the time. She was going to have to go back to the U.S.

Goodbye can sometimes be one of the hardest words we say. Sometimes we just don't understand why God works the way He does.

"Father, I give my dreams to You," Elinor prayed. She left, and the Kimyal tribe had no missionary.

But the Kimyal leaders were strong in their trust in Christ and their understanding of the Word of God. Even though they didn't have the Bible in their own language yet, they

continued to teach their people. More and more people trusted in Christ.

God is at work, even in the times we don't understand.

***

For though I am absent in body, yet I am with you in spirit, rejoicing to see your good order and the firmness of your faith in Christ.
Colossians 2:5

Lord, I see that even when circumstances don't make sense, You are still working. Help me to trust You even in the middle of confusing and difficult circumstances.

DAY 69

George and Sarah Boardman left for Southeast Asia as missionaries when Sarah was only twenty-one and George was only twenty-three, just two weeks after being married.

When people think about giving an offering to the Lord, they usually think about money. But George and Sarah didn't have any money to give. What they had was their time and their lives. It took a lot of their time to travel to Southeast Asia, learn the language and then set up a place to teach the people. They traveled long distances and spent a lot of time trying to understand the culture. They gave their lives because they knew the Kingdom of God and proclaiming the gospel was more important than their own health and comfort.

When you think about giving to God, money isn't the only thing to think about. Think about giving your time. Think about giving your life.

***

But I do not account my life of any value nor as precious to myself, if only I may finish my course and the ministry that I received from the Lord Jesus, to testify to the gospel of the grace of God. Acts 20:24

Loving Father, help me to serve You the way George and Sarah Boardman did, not out of duty, but out of love and joy and a desire for others to know You. Help me to want to give my life to You.

Way out in the middle of nowhere in a tiny village in Colombia, a woman had a strange dream. In the dream, a man she had never seen before came to her house and asked her to call her neighbors. He told all of them about something wonderful he called the *evangelio*. She had never heard this word before and didn't know what it meant.

For some time the woman pondered her strange dream. Then one day there was a knock at the door. . . .

It was the man in her dream. Her face went white, and she could hardly grasp what he was saying. But he asked her to call her neighbors, and she did. Then, sure enough, he preached about something called the *evangelio*. He said it meant "good news." He told them about Jesus, and every single one of those people came to Christ, including the woman who had the dream.

***

Your way, O God, is holy. What god is great like our God? You are the God who works wonders; you have made known your might among the peoples. Psalm 77:13-14

Dear God, thank You that You love to show Your mighty works among many different people groups. Thank You for showing Yourself mighty to save!

DAY 71

Joy Ridderhof's ministry, Gospel Recordings, sent out recordings all over the world. But Joy said to her team, "I want to start giving the recordings away instead of charging for them."

"But we already charge just enough to cover our expenses," someone said.

"These are people with almost no money," Joy answered. "I think we need to trust God to provide instead of charging."

So the team began to give the records away. When they didn't have any funds to ship the records out, they prayed and rejoiced. They praised God for what He had done and what He was going to do.

By the end of that year, the accountant said, "Without charging for the records, and without going into debt, we were able to send out twice as many records as we have before."

You can trust God to care for you too, as long as you're walking in the path He has called for you.

***

In all things I have shown you that by working hard in this way we must help the weak and remember the words of the Lord Jesus, how he himself said, "It is more blessed to give than to receive." Acts 20:35

Father, you love to provide for Your people in miraculous ways. I can always trust You to provide for me. Help me to always walk in that path of faith.

DAY 72

When Fanny Crosby was thirty years old, the terrible plague of cholera struck New York City where she lived. Five hundred people died every week. Fanny helped as much as she could, trying to remember words of comfort her own grandma had spoken long ago, so she could encourage dying children.

But the horror around her was overwhelming. After the plague ended, Fanny sank into a deep depression.

Finally, someone invited her to a church meeting. There the Lord spoke to Fanny's heart. She realized, "I have been trying to hold the world in one hand and the Lord in the other."

She had wanted to be a Christian, of course, but she also wanted the fame and glory that came from accomplishments.

Have you tried to do that? Have you wanted to be a Christian while at the same time receiving fame and glory for yourself? It doesn't work.

***

No servant can serve two masters, for either he will hate the one and love the other, or he will be devoted to the one and despise the other. Luke 16:13

Lord Jesus, help me to see any ways I'm trying to hold You at the same time that I hold the world. Help me to let go of the things of the world and just hold onto You.

DAY 73

The song that touched
Fanny Crosby's heart at that church
meeting was this one:

Alas and did my Savior bleed?

And did my Sovereign die?

Would He devote that sacred head

For such a worm as I?

The last verse says,

But drops of grief can ne'er repay

The debt of love I owe

Here Lord I give myself away

Tis all that I can do.

Then Fanny knew what she should do. "Lord, I give myself away! I give myself to You completely!" Fanny Crosby felt her soul filled with heavenly light and knew that her life had been changed forever.

Our Lord and Savior gave His blood and His very life for us. No amount of tears or good works would ever be enough to repay

Him for what He has done. He doesn't even want to be repaid—He has given Himself gladly to rescue you. He asks for you to give yourself completely to Him.

***

For all have sinned and fall short of the glory of God, and are justified by his grace as a gift, through the redemption that is in Christ Jesus, whom God put forward as a propitiation by his blood, to be received by faith. Romans 3:23-25

Lord Jesus, thank You so much that You were willing to give Your precious blood for us that we could receive salvation! Help me to always live in light of the great salvation You have provided.

DAY 74

When Margaret Laird visited the leprosy colony in Sibut, she saw many people whose bodies were deformed by the terrible disease. But one woman barely even looked like a person.

"Oh, Mama, don't look at me that way," the woman said. "I'm glad I got leprosy."

Mama was shocked.

"Years ago, you came to my village on your bicycle to tell us about Jesus," the woman continued. "But I spat on your shadow. I was the beautiful wife of the chief, and I didn't care anything about your Jesus.

"Then I got leprosy, and everyone turned me out of the village. I came to this leprosy colony and poured out my bitterness to Kongi. When he told me about Jesus, and about the big Mama on the bicycle, I remembered you.

"Now I've trusted in Jesus, and I know His grace and love and peace," said the woman. "So I thank God I got leprosy."

***

It is good for me that I was afflicted, that I might learn your statutes. The law of your mouth is better to me than thousands of gold and silver pieces. Psalm 119:71-72

Thank You, Lord, that You can use difficult circumstances to turn people's hearts to Yourself.

"The Kimyals need the Bible in their own language, Lord," Rosa Kidd prayed. "But I can't do it. I can't."

Phil Masters had started the translation, but he had been killed. Elinor Young had worked on the translation, but she had to leave because of sickness.

"I'll make so many mistakes," Rosa prayed. "It will be less than Your Holy Word."

Have you ever felt God calling you to do something that seems too hard?

"Rosa," God's voice said. "This isn't about you. This is about Me."

He spoke through Exodus 3:12:

"But I will be with you, and this shall be the sign for you, that I have sent you: when you have brought the people out of Egypt, you shall serve God on this mountain."

"Yes, Lord," Rosa said. She gazed at the huge mountains of Papua, Indonesia. "I surrender all of me to do Your will. I know You'll give me strength to do what You've called me to do." Rosa trusted God to help her with a work that seemed too hard, believing God would do a great thing. She knew she and the Kimyal people together would serve God on that mountain.

***

Dear Lord, I know You may call me to do something that seems too hard for me. Help me to trust You as I walk in faith, by the power of Your Spirit.

DAY 76

In Iran in 1990 thousands of secret house churches were meeting all over the country. Then the Iranian government discovered some of them and killed some pastors.

All over the world Christians began to pray for the Christians in Iran. Iranian Christians wrote letters and signed their names with their blood. "We're ready to stand together in Christ till the very end. We're ready to give our lives."

One pastor preached, "Where the blood of the saints has fallen, the church of the saints will grow! A church that is not afraid of death will never be defeated!"

More pastors were killed. But Muslims came to these Christians, whispering, "How is Christianity so strong that you're willing to peacefully give up your lives for it? I want something that real!"

Do you want something that real? God is as real in English speaking countries as He is in the Middle East. He delights to show Himself to be powerful.

***

Beloved, do not be surprised at the fiery trial when it comes upon you to test you, as though something strange were happening to you. But rejoice insofar as you share Christ's sufferings, that you may also rejoice and be glad when his glory is revealed.
1 Peter 4:12-13

Lord, thank You for showing Your power. Show Your power here in my country the way You're doing in the midst of persecution in the Middle East.

In 1994 the Communist revolution forced missionaries to leave Colombia. But Russell Stendal stayed and began to broadcast radio programs about truth and love and hope in Jesus.

"He is weak to preach that garbage about love," some revolutionaries growled. But others felt that the hatred and terrorism would destroy them. How desperately they needed those words of hope. Russell preached,

"Jesus said in John 8:12 'I am the light of the world. Whoever follows me will not walk in darkness, but will have the light of life.'"

Maria Fernandez, a well-known radio announcer for the revolutionaries, secretly listened to Russell's words of hope. Finally she also left her wicked way of life to follow Jesus. She even became a radio announcer for the Christians! She had thought the way of love was weak, but she found it was the strongest of all.

The wicked may seem stronger right now. But they're walking in a way of darkness and destruction that will destroy them. The true way of strength, hope, and light is to be found in Jesus.

***

Heavenly Father, I know that the way of love and hope is through Jesus Christ. Thank You for showing that through Your great salvation.

Joy Ridderhof and her friend Ann traveled to the Philippines to make gospel recordings for tribal people. One missionary couple was especially excited. "Our people have practiced for weeks to sing for the recordings! We've been praying over this for months!"

But Ann couldn't get the recording equipment to work. Joy prayed and rejoiced, but it never worked. The missionaries were so disappointed they cried.

The last day, Joy spoke to the people. "After Lazarus died, Jesus told Martha, 'If you will believe, you will see the glory of God.' If we believe, we'll also see the glory of God."

Joy and Ann took a ship to the next city, where their recording equipment was repaired. There they met some students who knew the tribal language and did a beautiful job making the recordings. They could finally ship records to the missionaries.

Life can be full of disappointments. But God still has a plan, and we can trust Him.

***

For you have been my help, and in the shadow of your wings I will sing for joy. My soul clings to you; your right hand upholds me. Psalm 63:7-8

Father, even in great disappointments You're still at work. Please remind me of this truth when I grow discouraged.

Amy Carmichael heard that terrible things happened to little girls in the Hindu temples. She dyed her skin brown and became a "Christian spy" to sneak into the temple, into the place where only Hindus were allowed, to find that all she had heard was true. She wrote the book *Things As They Are* to tell the Christians of England the truth about India.

"It's good you don't have blue eyes," a friend said. "They would have known you weren't Indian for sure."

Then Amy remembered a childhood prayer request—she had wanted blue eyes like her mother. How thankful she was now that God hadn't answered that prayer!

God might say "no" to you about something you're asking for. But He has a far bigger and greater plan than you can even imagine. The thing you might like to be different may be what God uses to bring souls to himself.

***

Delight yourself in the LORD, and he will give you the desires of your heart. Commit your way to the LORD; trust in him, and he will act.
Psalm 37:4-5

Thank You, Father, that even when it seems like I'm not getting the desires of my heart, I can trust You that You have a bigger plan and You know best.

Margaret Laird was sure God was telling her she needed a real hospital, not just a clinic, in the town of Ippy in the Central African Republic. But her mission organization's leaders didn't agree.

"Do you understand how much money that would cost?" they asked. "We're a *faith* mission. We can't afford that! And do you understand that we would have to ask doctors to become missionaries? Real doctors who have gone to school to study medicine for years?"

Yes, Margaret understood. She also knew her own husband, who had studied engineering, had given his life in missions. And didn't God own all the money in the world?

"If someone gives money for the hospital, will you save it in a special fund?" Margaret asked respectfully. The men agreed.

Margaret trusted the Lord that if He wanted that hospital, He would provide for it. And he did, in spite of what her authorities thought.

***

Jesus said to her, "Did I not tell you that if you believed you would see the glory of God?" John 11:40

Dear Lord, thank You that You own all the riches in the world! Thank You that we can trust You to provide for everything You want us to do.

One day a big game hunter lay in a hospital bed in Ippy reading a newspaper. "Madame Laird," he said, "if you'd do what the Pope does, you'd have had plenty of money for your hospital. He sells indulgences, so people can get their sins forgiven, and there's money to build the great cathedral. A good idea, no?"

Margaret began to cry. "Can you imagine worshiping a god who sold the right to sin?" she said. "If I believed we could buy God's forgiveness, I never would have come to Africa. What chance would these poverty-stricken Africans have? But God made the way of salvation the same for Africans as for me—and you. No matter how much money you have, you must come to Christ the same way any lowly servant comes."

As the wealthy hunter thought about her words, tears came to his eyes. "I see what you mean," he said. That day, he came to Christ.

***

The rich and the poor meet together; the LORD is the maker of them all. Proverbs 22:2

Thank You, Lord, that the ground is level at the foot of the cross, and everyone has to come to Christ the same way, in simple faith. Thank You that Your salvation doesn't depend on riches or good works, but on the work that Jesus has already done.

DAY 82

After many years, Rosa Kidd had finished the translation of the New Testament for the Kimyal tribe. Now, in 2010, the boxes of New Testaments would soon arrive on the little airplane.

Many of the missionaries came back from the U.S. for the event. After nineteen years, Elinor Young, who had been forced to leave because of sickness, returned too. She got to spend time, rejoice, and fellowship with her brothers and sisters in the Kimyal tribe, thanking God for bringing them the New Testament.

Hundreds of Kimyal Christians celebrated for days and days, with a huge pig roast feast and all their best food for the visiting missionaries. Then when the airplane arrived, they dressed in their finest tribal party clothes for the Bible party parade.

When we're celebrating the great things God has done, celebrating is very pleasing

to Him. Our God wants us to celebrate the good things He gives us. It's one way to praise Him!

***

Your righteousness, O God, reaches the high heavens. You who have done great things, O God, who is like you? Psalm 71:19

Thank You, Lord, for rejoicing with us when we rejoice! Thank You for giving us truly wonderful things to rejoice over.

DAY 83

Siud, the Kimyal church leader, could hardly believe it. For so many years, he had studied the Bible in other translations, and now he was holding a box of Kimyal New Testaments in his hands! He called for quiet, and prayed loudly.

"O my Father, my Father! The Promise that you gave Simeon that he would see Jesus Christ and hold Him in his arms before he died—I also have been waiting under that same promise, O God! You looked at all the different languages and chose which ones will be put into Your Word. You thought that we should see Your Word in our language. Today, You have placed it here in our land. And for all this, O God, I give You praise."

Rosa Kidd said, "We've had the Word of God in English for so long, we take it for granted. We don't realize what a precious gift we hold in our hands."

***

For Isaiah says, "Lord, who has believed
what he has heard from us?" So faith
comes from hearing, and hearing through
the word of Christ. Romans 10:16-17

O Lord, thank You for the encouragement
of seeing tribal people rejoice to have the
Bible in their own language! Help me to
remember what a privilege it is to have it
in mine.

DAY 84

In 1990 in Iran, thirteen-year-old Rashin Soodmand's father Hossein Soodmand was martyred. Rashin and her friends prayed about how they could secretly spread the gospel. They knew all the Bibles were being destroyed, so they decided to write out Scriptures on paper and leave them around the city.

With their one precious Bible, Rashin and her friends spent hours writing out Bible verses. Then they left the papers here and there around the city—on restaurant tables, in restrooms, in taxis.

Years later Rashin went to England to study the Bible. "Please God, we need more Bibles for the Muslim people," she prayed. Later Rashin began to teach the Bible over satellite. Thousands of Iranians have heard her gentle voice and true words.

By 2013, Rashin reported, "The Iranian people now have a million New Testaments.

Pray for the second million. The Muslim people of Iran already believe Jesus is a prophet. They love finding out more about Him."

***

And we also thank God constantly for this, that when you received the word of God, which you heard from us, you accepted it not as the word of men but as what it really is, the Word of God, which is at work in you believers. 1 Thessalonians 2:13

Thank You, Lord, for the written Word of God. Thank You that I can have my own copy and don't need to keep it a secret. Thank You that I can read it and learn about You.

DAY 85

At the Annual Assembly in the Karen tribes of Southeast Asia, the Christians came from all over the area with the best of whatever they had—which wasn't much. They didn't need an expensive sound system or comfy chairs—they met in a large round building on stilts with a thatched roof, and they sat on wooden benches or the dirt floor.

The important thing for them was that they were coming to worship God together and to encourage one another. Sometimes it got lonely with only a few Christians in each village. But the gathering for the Annual Assembly was always an encouraging time for all of them.

You can gather with other Christians too, and encourage each other in His Name. If you don't have Christians in your life to encourage you, you can ask God to bring them to you. If you do, thank Him for them!

***

Then those who feared the L ORD spoke with one another. The L ORD paid attention and heard them, and a book of remembrance was written before him of those who feared the L ORD and esteemed his name.
Malachi 3:16

Lord, thank You that Christians can encourage each other in their love for You and their service for You. Please help me to be an encourager to others.

Ana was a Colombian woman who felt like she must have demons. Murderous and evil thoughts kept coming in her head, and sometimes she went into terrible rages. Many people tried to help her, but she got no help.

Then one day Ana got a radio. On it she heard Russell Stendal telling about who Jesus really is. She had never heard this good news before, and the more she listened, the more she understood and believed. She prayed that she could meet Russell in person.

One day her prayer was answered. Russell himself passed in front of her house, talked with her, and gave her a Bible. Ana read it and read it. She trusted in Jesus, and soon, the evil thoughts were gone!

Ana wanted to tell everyone what Christ had done for her. Just like Mary Magdalene, she praised Him for delivering her from demons and gave the gospel fearlessly.

***

And the twelve were with him, and also
some women who had been healed
of evil spirits and infirmities: Mary, called
Magdalene, from whom seven demons
had gone out. Luke 8:1-2

Thank You, O Lord, that You deliver people
from demons. Thank You that You deliver
people from sin. Show me more of that
deliverance, I pray.

DAY 87

One day in 1963 when Joy Ridderhof was traveling and speaking about her life of faith and rejoicing, she received a telegram from back home in California. "We have only a week to buy the land we need," her team told her. "And the cost is $30,000." What a terrible lot of money!

"Follow the Jericho pattern," Joy wrote back. What did she mean?

Her team understood. They began praying two hours every day for the next seven days. Day after day went by without money, but they kept praying. On the fourth day they all read the verse that said, "In three days you will possess the land." They trusted God.

On the fifth day came a telegram. "A Christian lady has died and has given all her money to Gospel Recordings." It was far more than the $30,000 they needed.

If you keep trusting God step by step in your life, you can see great prayers answered too.

***

By faith the walls of Jericho fell down after they had been encircled for seven days.
Hebrews 11:30

Thank You, Lord, that You brought down the walls of Jericho in the Old Testament. Thank You that You work in miraculous ways in the lives of Your people today.

Fanny Crosby traveled to many places to tell the story of the love of Jesus for those who were lost. Once, at a rescue mission, she said, "Is there a young man here who has wandered from his mother's home and teachings?" Sure enough, a young man came to her and was saved that night. Afterwards Fanny wrote this song:

Rescue the perishing, care for the dying,

Snatch them in pity from sin and the grave.

Weep o'er the erring one, lift up the fallen,

Tell them of Jesus, the mighty to save!

Maybe people in your life are teaching you the truth, but maybe you feel like you might want to wander away from their teachings because the Christian life seems uninteresting. Notice the warnings in Fanny's words: *perishing, dying, sin, grave.* This is where the ways of sin will lead. Trust in Jesus to lead you in the way of truth and light.

***

There is a way that seems right to a
man, but its end is the way to death.
Proverbs 14:12

O Lord, help me to walk in the way of
truth and light and help others who are on
the wrong road, to tell them of Jesus, the
mighty to save.

DAY 89

Forty years after Fanny wrote the gospel song "Rescue the Perishing," she spoke at a meeting where she told the story about the young man at the rescue mission. Afterwards, an old man came up to her.

"That was me you were talking about, Miss Crosby," he said. "I was that young man who came to you that night. The Lord really did save me that night, and my life turned around. I've been living for Him ever since."

When you continue in faithfulness to God, giving out the gospel where He wants you to, you may not see people come to the Lord right away. You might see some people struggling with their faith. When people claim to trust in Him, you might wonder if it's real. But keep sowing the seed, like the sower in Matthew 13, asking the Lord to bring forth fruit from it, and He will faithfully do so. Continue in faithfulness to Him.

***

Those who sow in tears shall reap with shouts of joy! He who goes out weeping, bearing the seed for sowing, shall come home with shouts of joy, bringing his sheaves with him. Psalm 126:5-6

Dear God, please help me to be faithful in my life so I can see results like this in my later years. Help me to keep on faithfully giving the gospel of Jesus Christ to others.

DAY 90

The Indian Christian Ponnammal traveled with Amy Carmichael and helped her rescue children. Then she helped at the children's home, buying supplies, overseeing the building projects, mixing medicines, and caring for sick children. She was a tremendous help in her loving service to her Savior.

But then Ponnammal got cancer. After months of pain, she died.

Everyone felt bitter grief at the loss of their friend. But Amy said, "Our funeral will be different from the hopeless Hindu funerals. They wail and cry because they have no hope, but we know that Ponnammal is free of pain, and we'll see her again." Instead of wailing, the children dressed in bright colors. They cried tears of sadness, missing their beloved friend and helper, but they knew they had hope, so they rejoiced.

"Death isn't a complete loss," said Amy, "but only a farewell until we see each other again on the other side." The Hindus had never seen anything like it.

***

But we do not want you to be uninformed, brothers, about those who are asleep [dead], that you may not grieve as others do who have no hope. For since we believe that Jesus died and rose again, even so, through Jesus, God will bring with him those who have fallen asleep.
1 Thessalonians 4:13-14

Dear Father, help me to remember that even though death may be painful, it isn't the end. Help me to remember that Christian believers who have died go to heaven to be with You.

Sometimes tragedies happen that we don't understand at all.

Phil Masters had trained for years and worked hard to bring the gospel to the Kimyal tribe. For five years he taught Siud and other Kimyals.

And then in 1963 a neighboring tribe stabbed him to death.

Sometimes tragedies happen that we just can't understand.

Phil's wife Phyliss and his children mourned. The other missionaries mourned. And the people of the Kimyal tribe mourned.

In 2010, almost fifty years later, Phyliss Masters returned to the Kimyal tribe for their Bible party when they received their first New Testaments. There she met some people from the Yali tribe, the same tribe who had killed Phil. They had walked in darkness when

they killed the missionary, but now many of them had come to Christ and were walking in the light. They thanked God for Phil's life and his sacrifice to bring the gospel to them, people who had never heard.

***

Then Jesus told his disciples, "If anyone would come after me, let him deny himself and take up his cross and follow me. For whoever would save his life will lose it, but whoever loses his life for my sake will find it."
Matthew 16:24-25

Lord, I know that sometimes bad things happen that I can't understand. But I'll trust that You are over all, and out of the terrible evil done by men You can still bring something good.

DAY 92

When the long-anticipated New Testaments arrived in the Kimyal tribe, Pastor Siud read from the book of Revelation,

After this I looked, and behold, a great multitude that no one could number, from every nation, from all tribes and peoples and languages, standing before the throne and before the Lamb, clothed in white robes, with palm branches in their hands, and crying out with a loud voice, "Salvation belongs to our God who sits on the throne, and to the Lamb!" Revelation 7:9-10

Phyliss Masters, whose husband Phil had been killed by the Yali tribe almost fifty years earlier, looked around at all the people on the mountain, rejoicing. "I'm so grateful we could be a part of this, Lord," she whispered.

But one young man from the Yali tribe called all the pastors together. He turned to Phyliss and said, "I read the book *Lords of the Earth* and learned that my tribe had killed

your husband." He began to sob. "We killed him, when he had only shown us love. I want to ask forgiveness for my people."

How would you feel if you were in this place?

Phyliss responded, "I never held bitterness in my heart toward your people. They were in darkness and didn't know the Lord. I'm so grateful to see the rejoicing that has come from the work Phil did."

***

Dear Lord, You work in different tribes and nations to bring them to Yourself. Thank You for the example of Phyliss Masters forgiving and loving even though her husband was killed.

In Iran, Padina feared that if she got a hole in her stocking, Allah could dangle her like a yo-yo in hell. She did her best to keep every single rule, hoping that Allah would give her peace and eternal life.

She watched the men in the Parade of Grief, beating themselves until they bled. With the other women, Padina wept and wailed, scratching her face till she bled, pulling out her hair, and beating her head on the floor.

These Muslims believed that they needed to punish themselves to get Allah to be pleased with them. They didn't understand that all the punishment had already been taken by Jesus Christ. They were hopeless, because they could never do enough. But they didn't understand that Jesus had done it all.

You can never do enough to please God. But you don't have to, because Jesus has done it all. This is a reason for great rejoicing!

***

He saved us, not because of works done
by us in righteousness, but according
to his own mercy, by the washing of
regeneration and renewal of the Holy Spirit,
whom he poured out on us richly through
Jesus Christ our Savior. Titus 3:5-6

Thank You, Lord Jesus, that salvation comes
by faith instead of works. Help me to live by
faith and rejoice in that truth!

Padina had tried to please Allah, but failed. She quit trying and became an ordinary Muslim, marrying and getting a job. But her cruel husband divorced her, and her mother was dying. Padina sank into deep depression and even wanted to kill herself.

One night Padina saw a new kind of program on Iranian television. The people sang, "Jesus is my light! Jesus is my light!" She had never seen people looking so happy. She called the number. "Why are all you people so happy?" she asked.

"I'm so glad you asked!" Pastor Hormoz Shariat answered. "It's because of Jesus Christ. He has taken all the punishment for our sins. He rose again from the dead so that we can have victory over sin through faith in Him."

At first Padina thought the devil was trying to trick her into turning away from Allah. But when her mother was healed through a

simple prayer to Jesus, they both became believers.

***

. . . The faith that is through Jesus has given the man this perfect health in the presence of you all. Acts 3:16

Help me to remember, Lord, when life is discouraging and disappointing, that You're still the powerful God. Thank You for ways that You show Yourself strong.

DAY 95

Simeon spoke these words when he held the baby Jesus in his arms.

"Lord, now you are letting your servant depart in peace, according to your word; for my eyes have seen your salvation."
Luke 2:29-30

But 1,800 years later, another man spoke those same words. George Boardman said them, lying on a mat at the edge of a river watching thirty-four new Karen Christians being baptized. George was very sick and died at that river, when he was only thirty years old. But he had his life in perspective and knew what was really important.

It's important for you to get your life in perspective too. What are really the most significant things in your life? Instead of focusing all your thoughts on yourself and your issues, think about your life compared with all of time and eternity. You can become more aware of the greatness of God.

You may want to do great things for God, but He wants your heart, your whole self. He may want you to do something that may seem insignificant but will fit into His great plan.

**

Lord, help me to have Your perspective, and count as important the same things that You say are important. Help me to see life through Your eyes.

DAY 96

Jeannine Brabon was supposed to speak to the men in the most dangerous prison in Colombia. "Lord, what do You want me to say?" she prayed.

Immediately the story of David and Mephibosheth came into her mind.

She stood up to speak before the prisoners, who were either scoffing, eager, or curious. She told how David wanted to show kindness to Jonathan's son, even though he was the grandson of David's enemy.

Mephibosheth was lame, and David could have had him killed. But instead, for Jonathan's sake, David showed him kindness and compassion, treating him like his own son.

"This is what Jesus does for us," Jeannine said. "We are the children of the enemy. Our hands are covered with blood. But Jesus

says, 'I will bring you into my family. You will be my own son. You can eat at my table.' Jesus says, 'Come.' "

Twenty of those prisoners wanted to come to Jesus. They wanted to know love like that.

***

For the Son of Man came to seek and to save the lost. Luke 19:10

Thank You, Father, that the stories in the Old Testament give hints to us about Jesus. Thank You that You show us Your great love through Him.

In 1965, Joy Ridderhof went back to the little village in Honduras to visit her old friends. She hadn't seen them for twenty-five years.

"This is the lady who first brought the gospel to us!" some Christians told others who didn't know who she was. Some told stories of hearing about Christ from her spiritual "children." So now they were her spiritual grandchildren!

One man said, "I was in the jail where you preached at Christmas time. I had heard of Jesus, but I had never heard the Good News till you told it. Now I tell it to everyone."

Joy saw that the six years of ministry from so long ago had borne much fruit. She rejoiced to see what God had done.

When you sow seeds of the gospel for Jesus Christ, you don't know what He's

going to do with them. But you can trust that He will bring forth fruit in His time.

***

He regards the prayer of the destitute and does not despise their prayer. Let this be recorded for a generation to come, so that a people yet to be created may praise the LORD. Psalm 102:17-18

Thank You, Lord, that when we sow seeds of the gospel, You are the one who helps them to take root and bring forth fruit. I pray that the seeds of the gospel in my own life will take root and bring forth fruit in me and through me.

DAY 98

Amy Carmichael wrote so many books about her work in India that many people in England learned about her and her mission work. Even British children wanted to help Amy's girls.

One Christmas Amy's children received a box of toys, with a note:

"My son Robin read about your work and saved his money all year to buy your children gifts. He sent them off, but the ship that was carrying them sank. Then I offered to let him buy more, but this time with the money I was going to use to buy his own Christmas presents. He thought it over quite soberly for a while, but when he came back to me his face was shining and he said, 'Mother, I want to do it! Let's hurry and go shopping again!'"

How would it feel to lose all the gifts you had saved all year to buy? Would you be willing to make such a sacrifice?

***

Each one must give as he has decided in his heart, not reluctantly or under compulsion, for God loves a cheerful giver.
2 Corinthians 9:7

Heavenly Father, help me to be a cheerful giver too. Help me to be willing to make sacrifices for You.

DAY 99

Margaret Laird opened the door of her little house in Ippy in the Central African Republic. "Panyaka! It's been so many years since I've seen you!"

"I'm glad to be back, Mama," said her visitor. "I want to live near your hospital and tell people about Jesus."

Margaret gave him a hug. "I remember when I first treated you at the clinic when you were a boy."

"Oh, Mama, can you ever forgive me?" said Panyaka. "I told you to shut your big mouth and stop talking."

"I wanted to use my big mouth to bite your head off!" laughed Mama. "But I shut it instead."

"No, you didn't!" said Panyaka. "You opened your mouth to tell me about the love of Jesus, and I'll always thank you for it."

Do you ever get frustrated with people you're trying to help? As long as you have opportunity, keep showing them Christ's love, and keep telling them about Christ's love.

***

And [pray] also for me, that words may be given to me in opening my mouth boldly to proclaim the mystery of the gospel.
Ephesians 6:19

Dear God, help me to be a bold witness for You, even when people make fun of me. Thank You for examples like Margaret Laird who continued speaking Your love even when it was hard.

DAY 100

The Karen people of Southeast Asia had legends that sounded a lot like some Bible stories. One legend said that after the first man and woman sinned, the greatest God, Yuwah, had gone far away and could never be reached. Now they had to obey the evil Mukawli and his servants, the nats.

But the missionary Alonzo Bunker told them Mukawli was the father of lies. "I tell you," he said, "that Yuwah is near, because His Son Jesus Christ came to live and die and rise again for you, to bear your sin and make the way clear to Yuwah."

Do you think the only people Satan deceives are in other lands? No, the father of lies is at work all over the world. He'll deceive even Christians if he can. He might whisper that God doesn't love you or that God's ways are useless. But you can be free from these lies in Jesus Christ.

***

[The devil] was a murderer from the beginning, and does not stand in the truth, because there is no truth in him. When he lies, he speaks out of his own character, for he is a liar and the father of lies. John 8:44

Lord God, help me to be able to recognize Satan's lies. Help me to believe and stand in Your truth.

DAY 101

In August of 1999, kidnaping, murders, bribery, and all kinds of violence were taking place all over Colombia. But 400 Colombian pastors came together, preparing for a huge prayer meeting. They asked forgiveness of one another and from the Lord.

The next week over 3,000 people came from all over the world to pray for Colombia. They prayed all night. Two nights later, the stadium that could hold 35,000 people overflowed. People had to stand outside, waiting for some to leave so that they could enter and pray.

People fell on their faces and wept, over their own sins, the sins of their families and the sins of their nation.

"We will see a new day in Colombia," one speaker declared. "The Spirit of God

will sweep over this nation with His great salvation through Jesus Christ."

What has been happening in Colombia has been remarkable. A great work of the Spirit is taking place. God is sending revival to that land.

***

Will you not revive us again, that your people may rejoice in you? Show us your steadfast love, O Lord, and grant us your salvation. Psalm 85:6-7

Mighty Savior, thank You that You send Your salvation to those who cry out to You! Thank You for sending revival to other lands. Send revival to our own land too, I pray.

FOR FURTHER READING

The stories in *101 Devotions for Girls from the Lives of Great Christians* are inspired by other books written by Rebecca Davis.

With Two Hands: Stories of God at Work in Ethiopia (Hidden Heroes #1).

The Good News Must Go Out: Stories of God at Work in the Central African Republic (Hidden Heroes #2)

Witness Men: True Stories of God at Work in Papua, Indonesia (Hidden Heroes #3).

Return of the White Book: True Stories of God at Work in Southeast Asia (Hidden Heroes #4).

Lights in a Dark Place: True Stories of God at Work in Colombia (Hidden Heroes #5).

Living Water in the Desert: True Stories of God at Work in Iran (Hidden Heroes #6).

With Daring Faith: A Biography of Amy Carmichael.

Fanny Crosby: Queen of Gospel Songs (Potter's Wheel Books #1).

Joy Ridderhof: Voice Catcher Around the World (Potter's Wheel Books #2).

George Mueller: Pickpocket to Praying Provider (Potter's Wheel Books #3).

Hidden Heroes Series
by Rebecca Davis

With Two Hands
Stories of God at Work in Ethiopia
ISBN: 978-1-84550-539-4

The Good News Must Go Out
True Stories of God at Work in the Central
African Republic
ISBN: 978-1-84550-628-5

Witness Men
True Stories of God at Work in Papua, Indonesia
ISBN: 978-1-78191-515-8

Return of the White Book
True Stories of God at Work in Southeast Asia
ISBN: 978-1-78191-292-8

Lights in a Dark Place
True Stories of God at Work in Columbia
ISBN: 978-1-78191-409-0

Living Water in the Desert
True Stories of God at Work in Iran
ISBN: 978-1-78191-563-9

CHRISTIAN FOCUS PUBLICATIONS

Christian Focus | Christian Heritage | CF4K | Mentor

Christian Focus Publications publishes books for adults and children under its four main imprints: Christian Focus, CF4K, Mentor and Christian Heritage. Our books reflect our conviction that God's Word is reliable and Jesus is the way to know him, and live for ever with him.

Our children's publication list includes a Sunday School curriculum that covers pre-school to early teens, and puzzle and activity books. We also publish personal and family devotional titles, biographies and inspirational stories that children will love. If you are looking for quality Bible teaching for children then we have an excellent range of Bible stories and age-specific theological books. From preschool board books to teenage apologetics, we have it covered!

**Find us at our web page:
www.christianfocus.com**

CF4 •K
Because you're never
too young to know Jesus